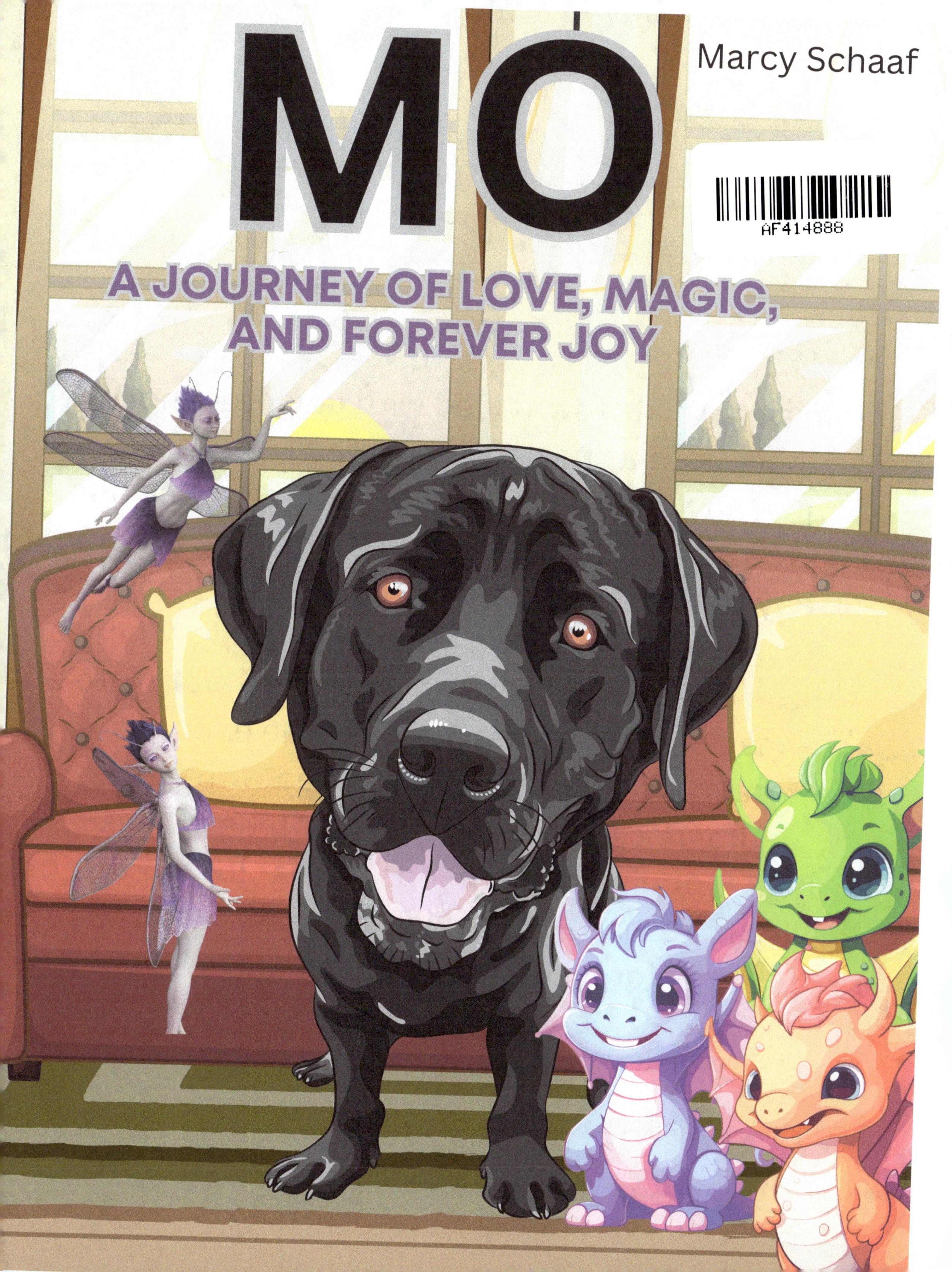

MO
Marcy Schaaf
A JOURNEY OF LOVE, MAGIC, AND FOREVER JOY
AF414888

Title: MO: A Journey of Love, Magic,
and Forever Joy

Intro:
In a charming town filled with laughter and love, there lived a special dog named Mo. Mo wasn't just any dog—he was kind-hearted, sweet, and loved to cuddle with everyone he met. But one day, something changed in Mo's world. Join us as we embark on Mo's Magical Journey, where a little dog's love transforms a simple story into a magical adventure. Discover the enchanted realm Mo finds himself in, filled with fairies, dragons, and everlasting happiness. This heartwarming tale reminds us that love and joy, like Mo's, have the power to create magic that lasts forever. Turn the page and let the enchantment begin!

MO:
A Journey of Love, Magic,
and Forever Joy

Once upon a time in the village of Badia Tedalda, Italy lived a sweet dog named Mo.
Mo was kind-hearted and loved to cuddle.

ITALY

One day, Mo felt a bit under the weather. Her nose was sniffly, and her tail didn't wag as usual.

Mo's family noticed she stopped eating and playing. Worried, they took her to the kind veterinarian, Dr. Lily.

Dr. Lily

Dr. Lily explained, "Sometimes, dogs get sick. They need rest, care, and love to feel better."

Mo's family showered her with love.
They made his favorite treats, hoping
Mo would find joy in them.

Despite their efforts, Mo continued feeling unwell. She grew weaker and stopped eating altogether.

One day, as Mo lay curled up,
something magical happened. A swirl
of sparkles enveloped her,
transporting her to a magical world.

In this enchanted land, fairies danced among flowers, and dragons soared through the clouds. Mo's tail started to wag, and her eyes sparkled with happiness.

Mo met a fairy named Sparkle, who said, "Welcome, Mo! Here you'll be happy and healthy forever."

Mo played with dragon friends and
ate magical treats that made her feel
stronger each day.

sugar bone
sugar bone
sugar bone

Back in the real world, Mo's family missed her dearly. They felt a warmth in their hearts, knowing Mo was in a special place.

sugar bone
sugar bone
sugar bone

Mo's family visited Dr. Lily, who assured them Mo was in a magical world where she'd be happy and healthy forever.

Mo's magical world continued to thrive, with fairies, dragons, and happy pets like Mo, who frolicked in eternal joy.

And so, Mo's story teaches us that even when our beloved pets leave, their love and joy linger in our hearts forever.

The end.

Mo the real life dog this story's about went with the fairy's and dragon's on December 13th 2023.

For more children's books visit:
www.BooksBySchaaf.com